United States
Department of
Agriculture

Forest Service

Pacific Northwest
Research Station

Research Paper
PNW-RP-586

March 2011

Stumpage Market Integration in Western National Forests

Jean M. Daniels

Authors

Jean M. Daniels is a research forester, Portland Forestry Sciences Laboratory, 620 SW Main, Suite 400, Portland, OR 97205.

Abstract

Daniels, Jean M. 2011. Stumpage market integration in western national forests. Res. Pap. PNW-RP-586. Portland, OR: U.S. Department of Agriculture, Forest Service, Pacific Northwest Research Station. 27 p.

This study presents results of statistical tests for stumpage market integration on 62 national forests in the Western United States. Quarterly stumpage prices from 1984 to 2007 obtained from cut and sold reports for USDA Forest Service Regions 1, 4, 5, and 6 (Northern, Intermountain, Pacific Southwest, and Pacific Northwest, respectively) were analyzed to establish the presence and extent of national forest timber markets. Statistical evidence suggests that prices from the Beaverhead-Deerlodge and Salmon-Challis Forests and the Kootenai and Idaho Panhandle Forests are linked and that only these two sets of forests can be modeled as integrated stumpage markets. Aside from these four forests, there is no evidence that the law of one price holds for national forest timber markets in the West.

Keywords: Stumpage prices, national forest timber, timber markets, cointegration, stationarity, arbitrage, integration.

Introduction

This research paper describes preliminary results of time-series analysis of stumpage prices on national forests in the Western United States. This analysis was completed as part of an effort to develop a spatially explicit stumpage price model for national forest timber in the Northern (Region 1), Intermountain (Region 4), Pacific Southwest (Region 5), and Pacific Northwest (Region 6) USDA Forest Service administrative regions. The objective of the model is to assist national forest planners in estimating the mix of sawtimber and nonsawtimber trees that will be sufficient to entice stumpage purchasers to buy sales designed for hazardous fuel reduction treatments, ecosystem restoration, and other forest management activities.

One preliminary consideration for model development is determining whether stumpage markets for national forest timber are linked. Linked markets have several implications for model development and purchaser behavior. Linkages determine whether national forests can be modeled as one effective market or several localized markets and the geographic extent of these markets. Market linkages also must be addressed when specifying regression equations used to test hypotheses pertaining to the model, or else parameter estimates may be biased. In addition, links among stumpage markets have implications for how changes in harvest flows in one forest can influence prices across several forests and associated private timberlands. Last, market linkages can provide clues about the nature of trading behavior among stumpage purchasers. Theoretically, competitive trade activity should ensure that prices of timber supplied by different forests tend toward uniformity, although short-run deviations may occur.

Market linkages are identified by examining trends in timber prices among forests. In general, markets that appear to be separate can be viewed as one effective market if their prices move together over time. The force that keeps these prices moving together is arbitrage, defined as the pursuit of opportunities to profitably move commodities across markets until price differences offset transaction costs. Arbitrage causes prices in different markets to converge spatially or temporally by encouraging people to buy low and sell high. Stumpage purchasers compete by using price arbitrage to actively exploit timber price differentials among forests. With efficiently linked markets, arbitrage opportunities are eventually exhausted and prices differ only by transaction costs. The law of one price (LOP) from international trade theory motivates this argument; it states that in long-run equilibrium, efficient arbitrage and trade activity ensure that the prices of homogeneous products supplied by different producers in different regions tend toward uniformity (Jung and Doroodian 1994).

1

Market linkages must be identified and accounted for if the stumpage market model is to be effective and useful. This preliminary report uses statistical tests to determine empirically if national forest stumpage prices are linked and, if so, the geographic extent of these linkages. Specifically, prices for 62 national forests in the Western United States were examined using correlation matrices, unit root tests for stationarity, and cointegration tests for market arbitrage. Tests reported here will be applied to enhance the national forest pricing model. Figure 1 shows the study area with regional and national forest boundaries delineated.

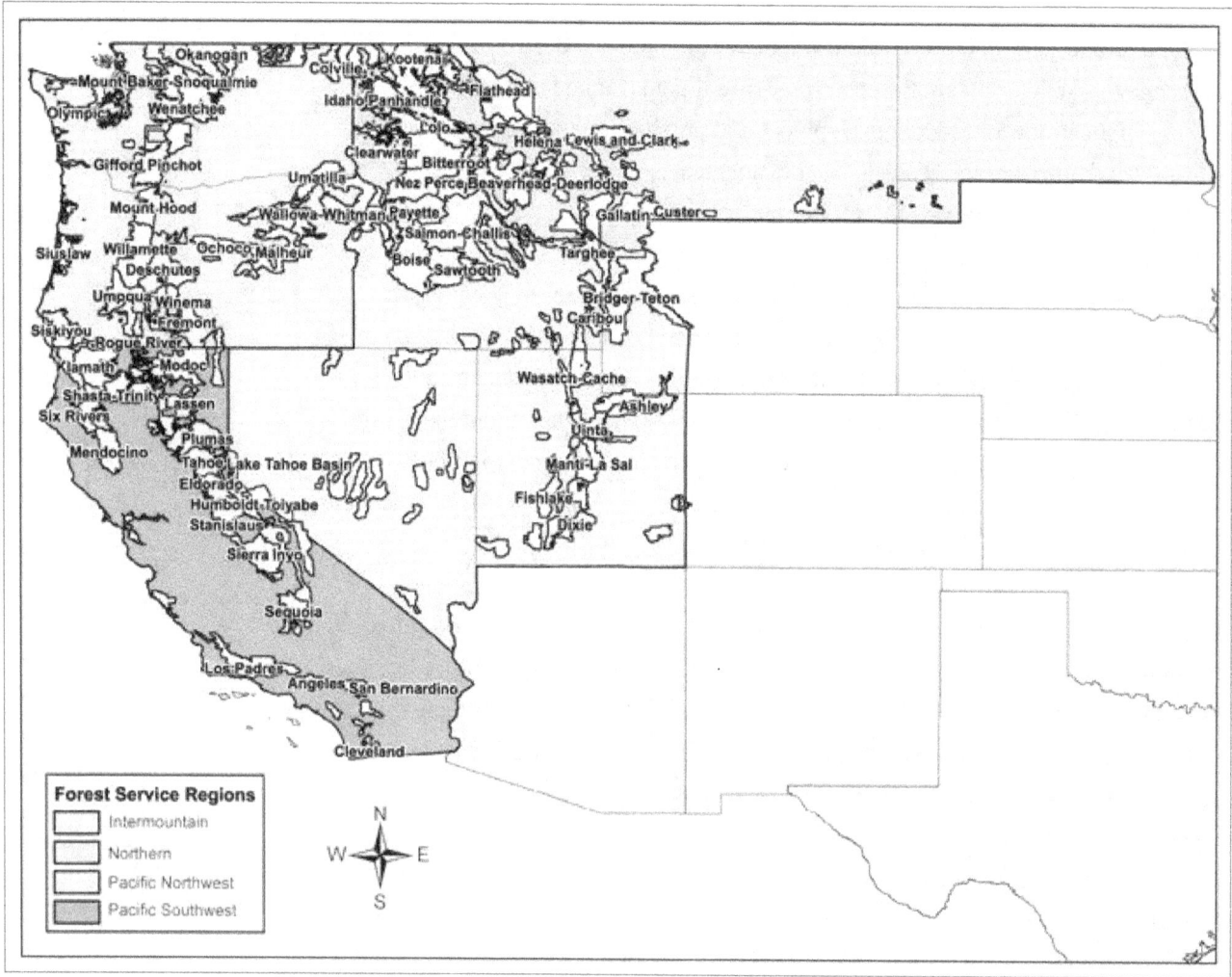

Figure 1—National forests of the Intermountain, Northern, Pacific Southwest, and Pacific Northwest Forest Service Regions.

Background

Many previous studies have examined price trends and integration in forest product markets with the methods used here. Cointegration analysis has been used to test for market integration, arbitrage, and the law of one price in a variety of forest industries. It is well-documented in the forest economics literature. In the United States and Canada, cointegration has been used to examine markets for softwood lumber (Baek 2006, Jung and Doroodian 1994, Murray and Wear 1998, Nanang 2000, Shahi et al. 2006, Stevens and Brooks 2003, Uri and Boyd 1990, Yin and Xu 2003). Generally, these studies examined the extent of integration in U.S. and Canadian regional lumber markets and how trade policies affecting softwood lumber have changed market structure over time. Other North American forest product industries have been tested for market integration as well, including pulp and paper (Alavalapati et al. 1997, Buongiorno and Uusivuori 1992) and newsprint (Tang and Laaksonen-Craig 2007). Cointegration analysis has also been applied extensively to study price movements, wood product market integration, price arbitrage, and the law of one price in forest industries in Europe. Studies performed in Europe generally investigate whether the easing of trade barriers in European Union member countries led to integrated and efficient roundwood markets (Hanninen 1998, Hanninen et al. 1997, Riis 1996, Stordal and Nyrud 2003, Thorsen 1998, Thorsen et al. 1999, Toppinen and Toivonen 1998, Toivonen et al. 2002).

Although the literature teems with studies examining integration in product markets, stumpage market integration studies are more rare. A few studies use cointegration to examine the link between stumpage and product markets (Luppold and Baumgras 1996, Luppold et al. 1998, Zhou and Buongiorno 2005). The remaining known studies of stumpage prices and market integration focus on the U.S. South (Nagubadi et al. 2001, Prestemon 2003, Prestemon and Holmes 2000, Yin and Newman 1996).

Stumpage markets have been modeled, usually for understanding and forecasting national and regional timber supply and demand. Past work assumed price equilibrium across spatial markets. Prestemon (2003) conducted an economic analysis for the Environmental Impact Analysis of the Biscuit Fire salvage operation, where the Siskiyou-Rogue, Klamath, and Six Rivers National Forests were treated as part of an integrated market. Integration was assumed because of proximity of the forests. Models such as the Timber Assessment Market Model (TAMM) and the Global Trade Model (GTM) also assume that timber markets are fully integrated (Binkley and Dykstra 1987). The TAMM model provides annual projections of volumes and prices in solid wood product and saw-timber stumpage markets by geographic region for up to 50 years (Adams and Haynes 1996). The U.S. West is assumed to comprise five regional markets but no tests were conducted for market integration. The GTM incorporates two U.S. supply regions (East and West) into a global market timber model, again without testing for integration.

I was unable to find any study testing for arbitrage behavior or integration in stumpage markets for the Western United States. In addition, no previous study has examined the geographic extent of markets for national forest timber or employed econometric methods such as unit root testing for price stationarity and cointegration analysis for long-run price relationships. Given the vast area of forest land in the Western United States and the traditional ties between federal timber sales and rural community stability and economic development, this finding was surprising. This study is the first known to examine market integration for national forest stumpage in the Western United States. Results reported here will be used to improve the accuracy of the spatial pricing model for national forest timber by incorporating cross-forest price relationships. The next section describes the data used for the analysis.

Data

Data were obtained from Kling (2008), who reported quarterly average sold prices for stumpage for the 62 national forests in Regions 1, 4, 5, and 6 between the first quarter (Q1) of 1984 and the first quarter of 2007. Sold prices are computed as volume weighted averages of high-bid prices for the right to harvest timber at a future date. Since 1984, sold prices have been reported as an all-species average of high bids, net of purchaser road credits and an allowance for timber stand improvements. Quarterly sold price series typically excluded sales with a total value of less than $2,000. Prices less than $1.00/thousand board feet (MBF) were omitted owing to the negative values generated from transformation to natural logarithmic form required for analysis. Prices were adjusted from nominal published prices to real 1984 dollars using the Producer Price Index.

Average sold prices by region over the study period are presented in figure 2. This figure illustrates the persistent price differences that have existed between regions for decades, although the price spread declined during the mid-1990s. Sold prices on all regions rose and then fell over time; prices in 2007 were either at or below prices in 1984. The price drop in the Pacific Northwest is especially dramatic. Timber prices in all four regions could be reacting to similar external drivers, suggesting linkages among the sold prices, which may scale down to integration at the forest level.

Tables 1 through 4 contain descriptive statistics for stumpage prices on each national forest by region from Q1 1984 to Q1 2007. At the forest level, median

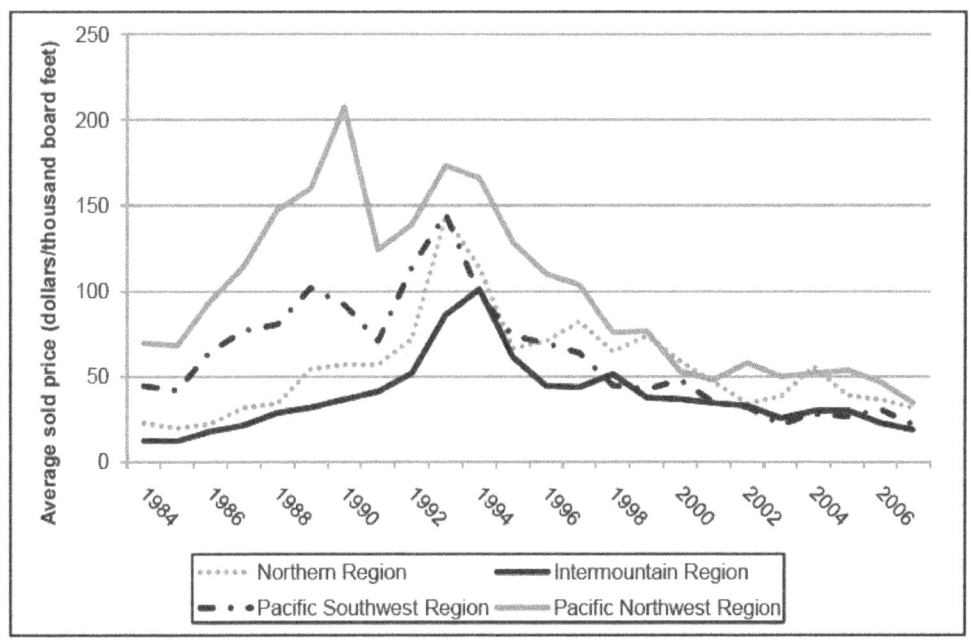

Figure 2—Median quarterly sold prices for timber harvests in the Northern, Intermountain, Pacific Southwest, and Pacific Northwest Forest Service Regions, 1984–2007.

values may provide a more accurate view of prices; averages may be skewed for forests with no timber sales for extended periods of time. Each forest has 93 quarterly price observations, but in many cases the minimum value was $0.00. In Region 1, the Clearwater, Idaho Panhandle, and Kootenai Forests had the highest median sold timber prices; prices on the Custer National Forest were far below the other forests. Prices were lowest for timber in Region 4 forests but were led by sales on the Payette. The Shasta-Trinity Forest had the highest sold prices in Region 5

Table 1—Descriptive statistics of sold prices for Northern Region timber by national forest, Q1 1984 through Q1 2007

Forest	Sample size	Mean	Standard error	Median	Standard deviation	Minimum	Maximum
			- - - - - - - - - - - - - *Dollars per thousand board feet* - - - - - - - - - - - - -				
Beaverhead-Deerlodge	93	47.47	5.13	27.24	49.49	4.89	292.09
Bitterroot	93	47.09	3.96	37.19	38.22	1.49	161.82
Clearwater	93	81.72	7.72	63.87	74.42	3.22	325.56
Custer	93	14.76	1.78	8.30	17.13	2.67	97.05
Flathead	93	62.94	5.41	45.79	52.21	0.92	254.99
Gallatin	93	28.12	3.36	16.20	32.39	2.05	175.09
Helena	93	42.67	5.57	19.85	53.76	1.91	276.17
Idaho Panhandle	93	90.53	6.19	81.64	59.66	10.84	347.89
Kootenai	93	105.13	7.56	92.68	72.90	7.41	371.54
Lewis and Clark	93	38.03	4.80	17.34	46.30	3.84	235.68
Lolo	93	65.85	5.96	52.40	57.49	3.45	265.56
Nez Perce	93	47.10	5.56	21.97	53.62	0.96	260.07

Table 2—Descriptive statistics of sold prices for Intermountain Region timber by national forest, Q1 1984 through Q1 2007

Forest	Sample size	Mean	Standard error	Median	Standard deviation	Minimum	Maximum
				Dollars per thousand board feet			
Ashley	93	29.00	3.43	14.96	33.11	3.66	177.20
Boise	93	68.03	7.57	44.43	73.04	0.00	398.35
Bridger-Teton	93	29.43	3.62	17.29	34.89	0.00	251.10
Caribou-Targhee	92	43.94	4.20	29.38	40.29	0.00	169.50
Dixie	93	32.22	4.31	9.24	41.54	3.97	204.86
Fishlake	93	37.76	3.74	23.53	36.06	5.45	145.57
Humboldt-Toiyabe	93	17.18	1.67	13.60	16.06	5.25	113.62
Manti-La Sal	93	19.72	3.99	8.01	38.43	0.00	301.44
Payette	93	88.56	10.29	62.91	99.22	0.00	509.82
Salmon-Challis	93	45.25	5.47	27.57	52.76	4.21	346.88
Sawtooth	92	18.54	1.97	12.51	18.91	0.00	128.09
Uinta	93	42.46	5.28	16.06	50.91	0.00	210.06
Wasatch-Cache	93	28.50	3.73	13.86	35.97	0.00	180.25

Table 3—Descriptive statistics of sold prices for Pacific Southwest Region timber by national forest, Q1 1984 through Q1 2007

Forest	Sample size	Mean	Standard error	Median	Standard deviation	Minimum	Maximum
				Dollars per thousand board feet			
Angeles	93	36.56	2.36	42.30	22.76	0.00	99.25
Cleveland	93	33.78	7.13	29.77	68.76	0.00	679.87
Eldorado	93	90.87	9.27	78.29	89.44	0.66	607.92
Inyo	93	48.52	6.25	25.72	60.30	0.00	330.57
Klamath	93	66.23	6.49	50.71	62.62	4.38	284.15
LTBMU[a]	93	23.95	2.47	17.67	23.87	0.00	125.60
Lassen	93	90.97	8.43	64.51	81.31	4.54	366.28
Los Padres	93	14.68	0.99	15.87	9.52	0.00	42.36
Mendocino	93	60.67	7.64	21.81	73.68	0.54	286.23
Modoc	93	94.65	12.74	29.71	122.89	0.62	558.58
Plumas	93	75.24	7.75	46.28	74.71	1.67	386.40
San Bernardino	93	26.43	1.53	28.99	14.80	0.00	72.78
Sequoia	93	55.58	7.92	26.06	76.33	0.00	419.92
Shasta-Trinity	93	112.69	11.10	91.76	107.04	4.11	533.00
Sierra	93	66.42	6.80	47.99	65.60	0.05	341.35
Six Rivers	93	87.10	8.47	60.46	81.72	2.63	335.89
Stanislaus	93	60.75	5.52	44.42	53.22	8.95	296.07
Tahoe	93	76.89	6.63	60.81	63.92	6.42	334.83

[a] Lake Tahoe Basin Management Unit.

Table 4—Descriptive statistics of sold prices for Pacific Northwest Region timber by national forest, Q1 1984 through Q1 2007

Forest	Sample size	Mean	Standard error	Median	Standard deviation	Minimum	Maximum
		- - - - - - - - - - - Dollars per thousand board feet - - - - - - - - - - - - -					
Colville	93	72.32	4.85	71.23	46.76	6.58	221.37
Deschutes	93	59.53	4.08	54.02	39.32	5.62	172.55
Fremont	93	91.21	8.32	65.35	80.22	0.00	378.97
Gifford Pinchot	93	111.22	10.13	89.54	97.66	3.16	389.43
Malheur	93	97.81	8.81	74.61	84.96	6.38	363.27
Mount Baker-Snoqualmie	93	80.87	8.24	53.35	79.47	0.00	362.91
Mount Hood	93	136.37	10.92	107.36	105.30	12.51	445.36
Ochoco	93	105.30	11.36	47.25	109.59	0.00	485.88
Okanogan	93	64.23	6.33	42.20	61.00	2.04	286.94
Olympic	93	80.13	6.54	62.88	63.04	4.89	261.96
Rogue River	93	127.39	12.84	99.64	123.85	6.71	679.62
Siskiyou	92	172.09	17.82	126.52	170.90	5.92	995.59
Siuslaw	93	134.58	9.83	110.41	94.82	12.69	462.75
Umatilla	93	48.74	4.22	38.50	40.73	0.00	220.23
Umpqua	93	150.09	13.95	116.53	134.55	13.57	698.67
Wallowa-Whitman	93	51.16	3.28	48.30	31.63	4.38	131.53
Wenatchee	93	47.05	4.25	35.08	41.01	6.74	285.80
Willamette	93	174.45	10.03	159.60	96.77	14.95	390.22
Winema	93	96.35	8.56	76.50	82.50	3.09	503.56

with the Eldorado Forest a distant second. Region 6 sold prices were the highest overall; timber on the Willamette, Umpqua, and Siskiyou Forests commanded the highest prices of the 62 study forests. The range of prices both within and between regions likely reflects species differences, proximity to manufacturing activity, and, in the Pacific Northwest, influence of price premiums in private log export markets (Daniels 2005). Unfortunately, the sold price series used in this report represents an all-species average and does not allow testing for species differences. The influence of manufacturing clusters on prices will be examined in the next stage of spatial pricing model development.

Stumpage prices from 2002 to 2007 for all 62 forests were averaged, sorted from highest to lowest, and grouped by quartiles. The resulting rankings by price are mapped by region in figures 3 through 6 with a color scheme that depicts price quartiles from lowest to highest. The same quartile groupings are used for all regions. The figures show that Region 4 forests tend to have the lowest timber prices and Region 6 prices are highest, especially forests in Oregon.

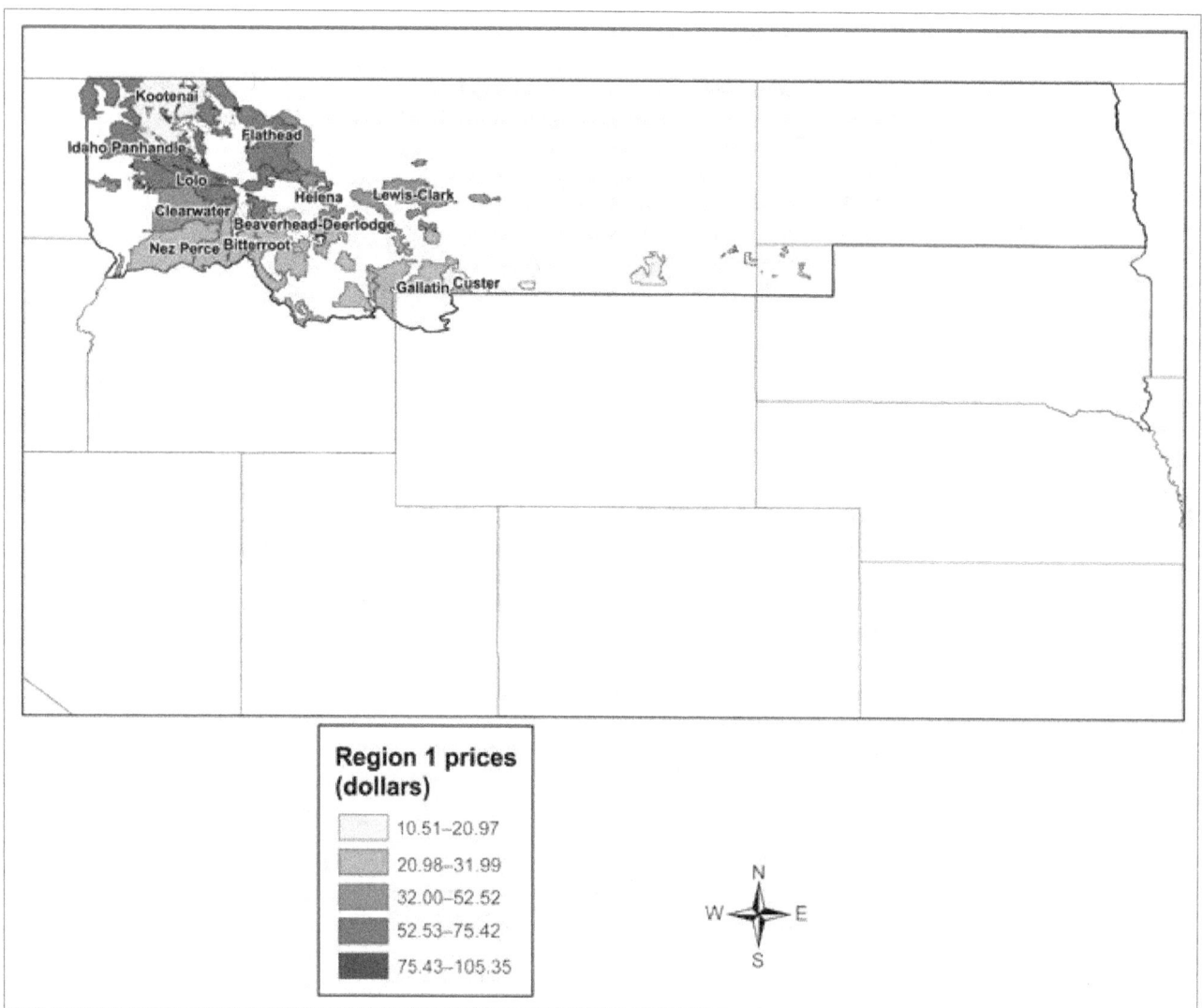

Figure 3—Stumpage price rankings for national forests of the Northern (Region 1) Forest Service Region.

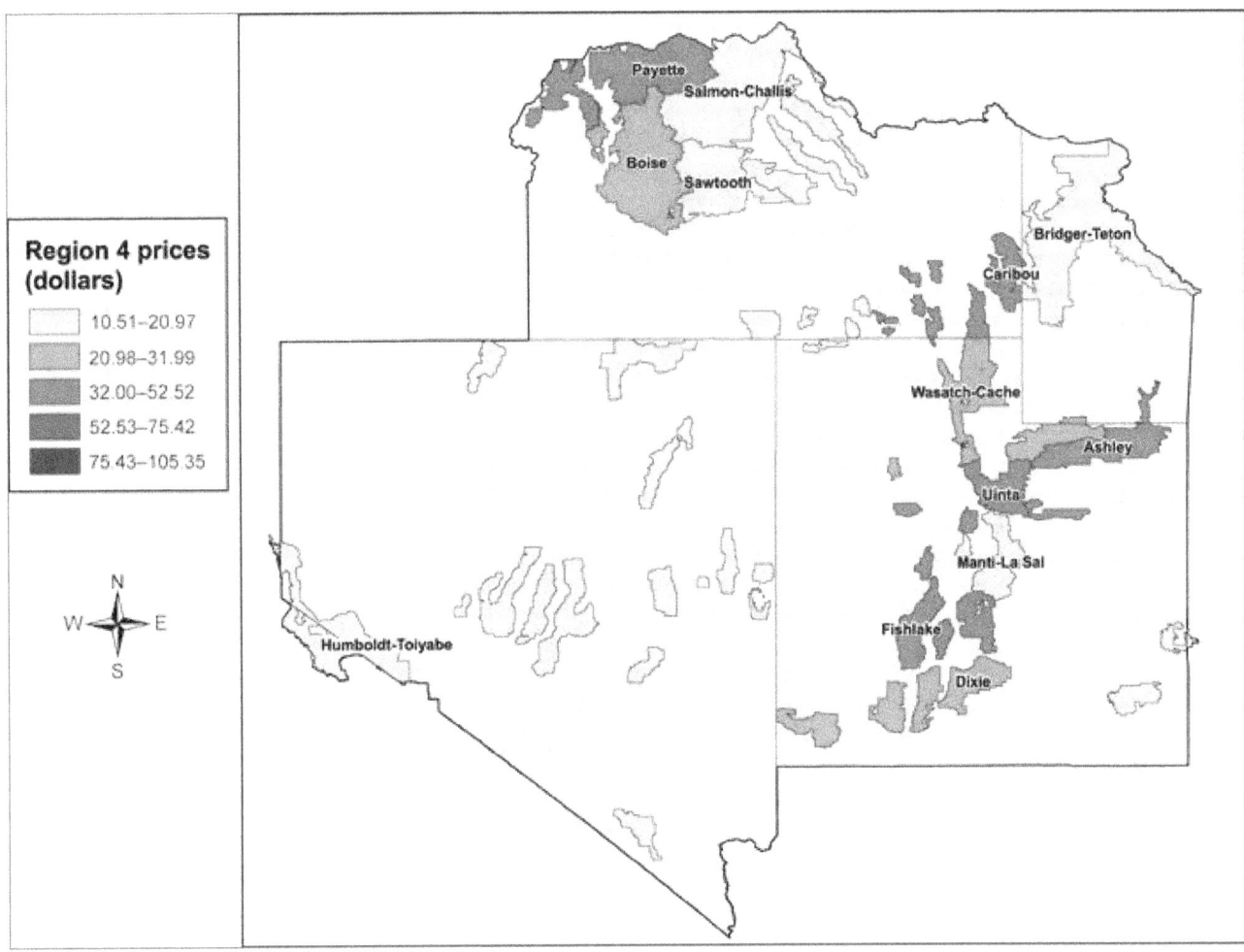

Figure 4—Stumpage price rankings for national forests of the Intermountain (Region 4) Forest Service Region.

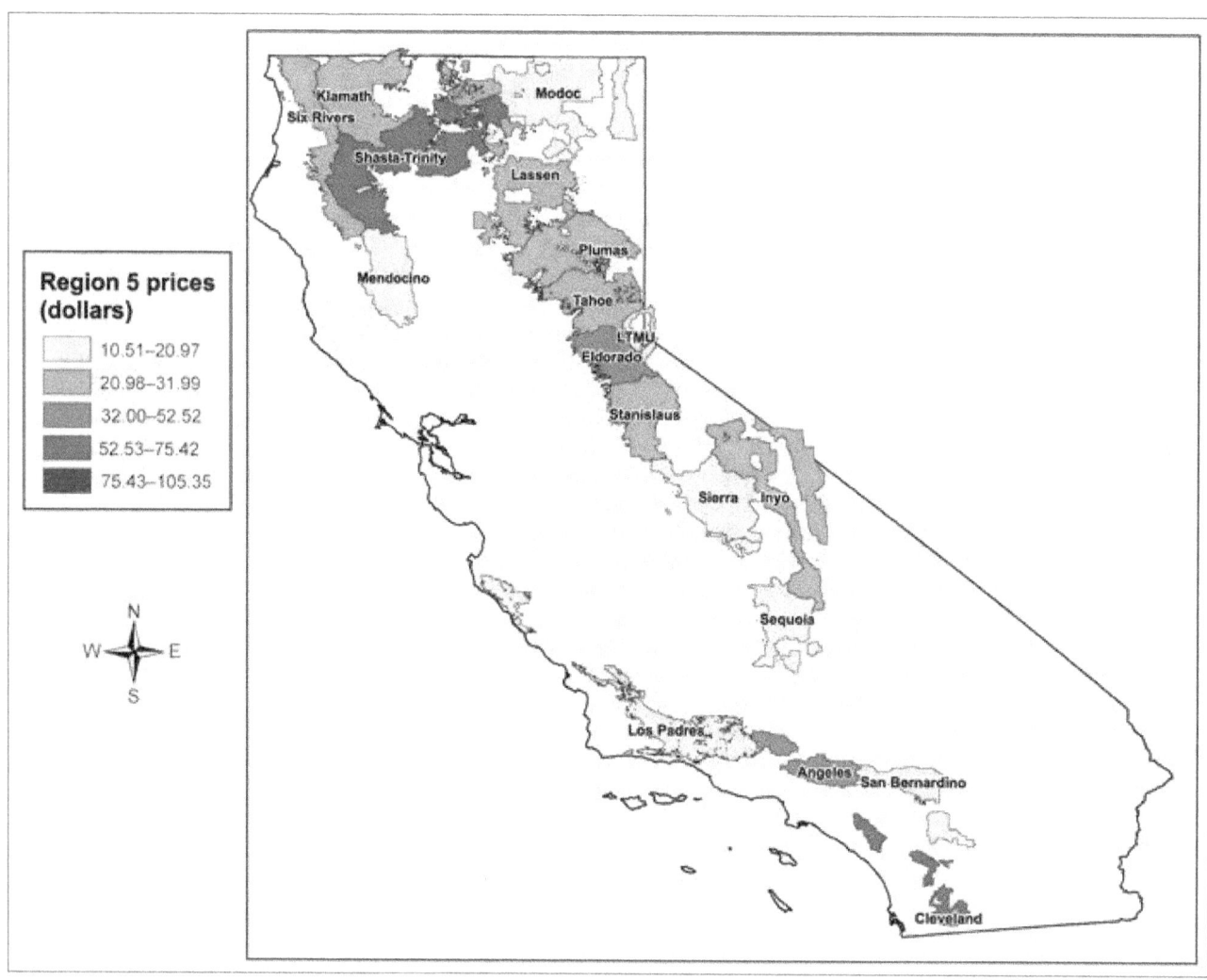

Figure 5—Stumpage price rankings for national forests of the Pacific Southwest (Region 5) Forest Service Region.

Figure 6—Stumpage price rankings for national forests of the Pacific Northwest (Region 6) Forest Service Region.

Methods

Empirical analysis to determine the extent of national forest timber markets began by looking for correlation among stumpage prices (Murray and Wear 1998, Yin and Newman 1996). Correlation matrices were developed for forests in each region (tables 5 through 8). Values near 1.0 or -1.0 suggest that prices have a strong positive or negative relationship, respectively; values near zero suggest very little or no relationship between prices. Values greater than 0.5 are shaded for emphasis.

Table 5—Forest Service Northern Region stumpage price correlation matrix

Forest	Beaverhead-Deerlodge	Bitterroot	Clearwater	Custer	Flathead	Gallatin	Helena	Idaho Panhandle	Kootenai	Lewis and Clark	Lolo	Nez-Perce
Beaverhead-Deerlodge	1.0000	0.3314	0.3413	0.1918	0.1351	0.0905	0.2141	**0.5860**	**0.5527**	0.3631	**0.5200**	0.1314
Bitterroot		1.0000	0.0869	0.0316	0.0173	0.1005	0.0927	0.0983	0.1761	0.1712	0.2311	0.1293
Clearwater			1.0000	0.1292	0.0458	0.1482	0.1463	0.4454	0.3673	0.3640	**0.5196**	0.2211
Custer				1.0000	0.0326	0.2205	0.1977	0.1958	0.2585	0.1558	-0.0019	-0.0384
Flathead					1.0000	-0.0225	0.2730	0.3590	0.1802	0.4131	0.1529	0.2465
Gallatin						1.0000	0.0905	0.2384	0.3400	0.2276	0.0212	0.0309
Helena							1.0000	0.2424	0.2859	0.2574	0.2416	0.3061
Idaho Panhandle								1.0000	**0.7060**	0.4840	**0.5466**	0.3004
Kootenai									1.0000	0.3826	0.4787	0.1402
Lewis and Clark										1.0000	0.3032	0.3999
Lolo											1.0000	0.2563
Nez Perce												1.0000

Correlation values greater than 0.5 are bold for emphasis.

Table 6—Forest Service Intermountain Region stumpage price correlation matrix

Forest	Ashley	Boise	Bridger-Teton	Caribou-Targhee	Dixie	Fishlake	Humboldt-Toiyabe	Manti-La Sal	Payette	Salmon-Challis	Sawtooth	Uinta	Wasatch-Cache
Ashley	1.0000	0.0718	0.1342	0.3064	0.0095	0.2773	-0.0315	-0.0406	0.1849	0.2953	0.3903	0.2440	0.2760
Boise		1.0000	0.4130	0.2153	0.0486	0.2539	-0.2399	0.2290	**0.5386**	**0.6149**	0.2941	0.2353	0.1486
Bridger-Teton			1.0000	0.3234	-0.0369	0.2368	0.0281	0.2154	0.4019	0.3394	0.1792	0.1827	0.1911
Caribou-Targhee				1.0000	0.1363	0.4734	-0.0770	0.2813	0.0746	0.3344	0.2556	0.3398	0.4187
Dixie					1.0000	0.0823	-0.0482	0.1703	0.0740	0.0568	0.3045	0.1836	0.0375
Fishlake						1.0000	0.0521	0.1141	0.0604	0.3700	0.2006	0.4067	0.3559
Humboldt-Toiyabe							1.0000	0.1258	0.0730	-0.1084	0.0006	-0.1053	0.0031
Manti-La Sal								1.0000	0.1705	0.0531	0.1407	0.2693	0.2627
Payette									1.0000	0.4893	0.1944	0.1441	-0.0428
Salmon-Challis										1.0000	0.3325	0.2510	0.2527
Sawtooth											1.0000	**0.5371**	0.3017
Uinta												1.0000	0.2823
Wasatch-Cache													1.0000

Correlation values greater than 0.5 are bold for emphasis.

Table 7—Forest Service Pacific Southwest Region stumpage price correlation matrix

Forest	Angeles	Cleveland	Eldorado	Inyo	Klamath	LTBMU[a]	Lassen	Los Padres	Mendocino	Modoc	Plumas	San Bernardino	Sequoia	Shasta-Trinity	Sierra	Six Rivers	Stanislaus	Tahoe
Angeles	1.0000	0.0623	-0.1992	-0.1667	-0.1323	0.1367	-0.3430	0.4368	-0.0639	-0.2594	-0.2375	-0.0194	0.0681	-0.0255	-0.1190	-0.3031	0.0110	-0.1906
Cleveland		1.0000	-0.0739	-0.2176	-0.3515	-0.1110	-0.3264	-0.1273	-0.4612	-0.1669	-0.2676	-0.2028	-0.4068	-0.2876	-0.2817	-0.1258	-0.2961	-0.2967
Eldorado			1.0000	0.2835	0.1209	0.3382	0.4431	0.0893	0.3741	0.0731	0.2327	0.3130	0.3747	0.1490	0.3049	0.4303	0.3574	0.4862
Inyo				1.0000	0.0504	0.2632	0.3337	-0.0390	0.2322	-0.0091	0.3528	0.1078	0.1426	0.1108	0.2650	0.3072	0.3942	0.2743
Klamath					1.0000	0.0933	0.4175	0.0611	0.1966	0.3648	0.4670	0.2004	0.4716	**0.6840**	0.4765	0.1434	0.3657	0.4407
LTBMU[a]						1.0000	0.0506	0.1651	0.1583	-0.0152	0.2944	0.2556	0.2958	0.2410	0.3005	-0.0201	0.3675	**0.5978**
Lassen							1.0000	-0.2353	0.3566	0.4173	**0.6869**	0.1846	0.4692	0.4057	**0.6857**	**0.5717**	0.3600	0.3684
Los Padres								1.0000	0.0533	-0.1569	-0.0567	0.0997	0.2079	0.0352	-0.0026	-0.1386	0.2005	0.1117
Mendocino									1.0000	0.1158	0.1084	0.4475	0.3101	0.2274	0.3357	0.4809	0.2749	0.2457
Modoc										1.0000	0.3636	0.0383	0.3495	0.3117	0.3143	-0.0045	0.1120	0.2928
Plumas											1.0000	0.2364	**0.5168**	0.4317	**0.5809**	0.2527	0.3575	**0.6015**
San Bernardino												1.0000	0.1639	0.1358	0.1303	0.1452	0.2409	0.4098
Sequoia													1.0000	**0.5665**	**0.6543**	0.1306	0.4986	**0.5678**
Shasta-Trinity														1.0000	**0.6265**	0.1611	0.4226	0.4349
Sierra															1.0000	0.4743	**0.5029**	**0.5133**
Six Rivers																1.0000	0.1407	0.4654
Stanislaus																	1.0000	0.2053
Tahoe																		1.0000

[a] LTBMU = Lake Tahoe Basin Management Unit.
Correlation values greater than 0.5 are bold for emphasis.

Table 8—Forest Service Pacific Northwest Region stumpage price correlation matrix

Forest	Colville	Deschutes	Fremont	Gifford Pinchot	Malheur	Mount Baker-Snoqualmie	Mount Hood	Ochoco	Okanogan	Olympic	Rogue River	Siskiyou	Siuslaw	Umatilla	Umpqua	Wallowa-Whitman	Wenatchee	Willamette	Winema
Colville	1.0000	0.0717	-0.0115	-0.0266	0.0153	0.1119	0.1592	0.0167	0.2928	0.1030	0.0760	0.2781	-0.0716	0.1706	0.1338	0.1071	0.0698	0.3150	-0.2189
Deschutes		1.0000	0.4230	0.2084	0.3187	0.3673	0.2953	0.3553	0.1009	0.3918	0.0752	0.0995	0.3219	0.1683	0.3319	0.0660	0.2836	0.1724	0.1986
Fremont			1.0000	0.4436	**0.6386**	0.4918	0.4967	0.4459	0.1162	0.4563	0.2625	0.0486	0.3247	0.2373	0.4374	0.3136	0.2469	0.3606	0.4088
Gifford Pinchot				1.0000	0.4240	0.2404	0.2785	0.3885	0.0338	0.3532	0.4248	0.1137	0.1668	0.1259	0.3387	0.3892	0.1218	0.2492	0.2524
Malheur					1.0000	0.4680	**0.5237**	**0.6031**	0.2892	0.4361	0.3716	0.0229	0.1660	0.2795	0.3801	0.2110	0.2425	0.3413	0.5229
Mount Baker-Snoqualmie						1.0000	0.2992	0.4088	0.1170	0.4092	0.3357	0.2160	0.2306	0.1657	0.3495	0.3973	0.2601	0.2518	**0.5206**
Mount Hood							1.0000	0.4202	0.3186	**0.5391**	0.3362	0.0839	0.1847	0.2644	0.4743	0.3218	0.1824	**0.5350**	0.3593
Ochoco								1.0000	0.1817	0.4192	0.1759	0.0745	0.1696	0.4553	0.1366	0.1235	0.2627	0.3037	0.4202
Okanogan									1.0000	0.3152	0.2778	-0.0480	-0.0401	0.2016	0.2879	0.1160	0.0834	0.4109	0.2322
Olympic										1.0000	0.4169	0.1438	0.2265	0.4346	0.3171	0.2058	0.4005	0.4660	0.3554
Rogue River											1.0000	0.2346	0.1917	0.1007	0.4829	0.3514	0.2527	0.4342	0.4341
Siskiyou												1.0000	0.1598	-0.1024	0.2083	0.1415	0.2233	0.2415	-0.0233
Siuslaw													1.0000	-0.0455	0.2336	0.0349	0.0960	0.0399	0.2235
Umatilla														1.0000	0.1057	0.1553	0.2816	0.3648	0.2196
Umpqua															1.0000	0.3047	0.2147	0.4018	0.4028
Wallowa-Whitman																1.0000	-0.0048	0.4188	0.3138
Wenatchee																	1.0000	0.3085	0.2441
Willamette																		1.0000	0.2936
Winema																			1.0000

Correlation values greater than 0.5 are bold for emphasis.

In Region 1, prices in the Beaverhead-Deerlodge, Idaho Panhandle, Kootenai, Lolo, and Clearwater National Forests show evidence of correlation. Figure 3 shows these forests are close to one another. Region 4 contains two groups of correlated stumpage prices: (1) the Boise, Payette, Salmon-Challis Forests and (2) the Sawtooth and Uinta Forests. Region 5 forests display another spatial trend; forests near the Sierra Mountains are generally correlated, as are forests in northern California. In contrast, a strong negative correlation exists between Angeles and Cleveland National Forest prices and most other Region 5 forests. Region 6 had few high correlation values; stumpage prices on the Malheur National Forest were modestly correlated with four other forests: Fremont, Mount Hood, Ochoco, and Winema.

Correlation matrices provide preliminary evidence of price relationships among some western national forests. However, correlation matrices do not provide sufficient statistical evidence of market integration. Tests for market integration are equivalent to testing to see if the law of one price holds using the arbitrage price condition:

$$P^1_t = \alpha + \beta P^2_t + \varepsilon_t \tag{1}$$

where P^1_t and P^2_t are prices in markets 1 and 2 and ε_t is the error term at time t. The constant term α represents transportation costs. If the LOP holds, arbitrage opportunities are exhausted and β is not significantly different from 1. Prices differ only by transportation costs.

Testing the arbitrage condition has traditionally been an important feature of empirical analysis of commodity markets. However, this price regression has some statistical problems that may invalidate conclusions based on the estimated parameters. Under the law of one price, prices are jointly determined in linked markets, making conventional estimation subject to simultaneity bias. In addition, if the two price series are nonstationary, conventional regression procedures fail to provide reliable parameter estimates. Thus, all price series must be tested for stationarity before undertaking further testing for stumpage market integration.

A price series is stationary when the mean, variance, and covariances of the series are constant over time and nonstationary when they are not. In a nonstationary series, observations are generated not only by independent random events, but also contain information left over from previous periods. As statistical properties are partly a function of time, the error terms are correlated and standard regression estimation and inference procedures are invalid. To illustrate, consider this time series process:

$$P_t = \rho P_{t-1} + \varepsilon_t \tag{2}$$

where P_t is the current period price, P_{t-1} is the previous period price (the first lag of variable P), ρ is a parameter to be estimated, and ε_t is the residual, assumed to be random. If $|\rho| \geq 1$, the process "explodes" in the sense that P will grow without bound as time approaches infinity. If $|\rho| < 1$, P is a stationary price series; a shock to the series would eventually result in a convergence back to a steady state. The closer it is to 1, the slower the rate of convergence. Serious problems occur if $\rho = 1$. The resulting model

$$P_t = P_{t-1} + \varepsilon_t \tag{3}$$

is a common example of a nonstationary series called a random walk and the model is said to have a unit root. In such a model, any shock to the series will have permanent effects and the variance increases with time. This model may be expanded by incorporating a constant and/or a deterministic time trend representing a normal rate of growth or decline over time. Any shock to the series will still have permanent effects in addition to a traditional drift in one direction.

Stationarity can often be achieved through differencing operations. A series is difference stationary if the first (or higher order) difference of the series is stationary. Using quarterly data, the first difference of P is a series generated by subtracting the previous quarter's price from each current period price:

$$P_t - P_{t-1} = \varepsilon_t \qquad \text{or equivalently } \Delta P_t = \varepsilon_t \quad . \tag{4}$$

Sometimes only one differencing operation is necessary to remove correlation in the error terms; sometimes additional differencing is necessary. The number of differencing operations (or lags) required to make the series stationary is the order of integration, denoted as $I(d)$. The original undifferenced series are called the levels. Thus, a time series is denoted $I(0)$ when it is already stationary in levels and $I(d)$ when it must be differenced d times to achieve stationarity owing to the presence of unit roots in the lags (Greene 2003). For example, the random walk above is difference stationary; the first difference of P is stationary, making it an $I(1)$ series.

There are two important considerations when testing for a unit root. The first is whether to include a constant, a constant and a time trend, or neither in the test equation. Including irrelevant regressors reduces the power of the test to reject the null hypothesis of a unit root. Another critical aspect is the choice of lag length to eliminate correlation in the error terms. Unit root tests were conducted using the Augmented Dickey-Fuller (ADF) unit root test, which allows for correlation at higher order lags (Dickey and Fuller 1979). The ADF test works by adding m lagged difference terms of P to the right-hand side of the test regression:

$$\Delta P_t = \alpha + \beta_t + \delta P_{t-1} + \lambda_1 \Delta P_{t-1} + \lambda_2 \Delta P_{t-2} + \ldots + \lambda_m \Delta P_{t-m} + \varepsilon_t \tag{5}$$

where α is a constant, β the coefficient on a time trend, $\delta = (\rho - 1)$, and m the number of lags required to remove correlation in the error terms (lag order). The ADF test is conducted under the null hypothesis of a unit root $H_0: \rho = 1$ and a one-sided alternative $H_1: \rho < 1$. The standard t-distribution of critical values cannot be used because the test is performed on the residual term. The ADF test statistic is the ratio of δ to its standard error. If this ratio is significantly different from zero, the null hypothesis is rejected.

Cointegration theory reconciles findings of nonstationarity with the possibility of testing relationships among prices. Cointegration is based on the idea that even if prices themselves are nonstationary, a linear combination of them may exist that is stationary. The stationary linear combination is represented by a cointegrating equation that may be interpreted as a long-run equilibrium relationship between prices. There may be co-movement between trending prices such that the prices will revert to a common long-run equilibrium relation. The existence of a stabilizing relationship among the series suggests a common fundamental force tying these series together. In this study, the hypothesized common force is market integration resulting from arbitrage behavior on the part of national forest timber purchasers.

After applying unit root tests, the Johansen maximum likelihood procedure was used to test for cointegration among nonstationary series (Johansen 1995). One advantage of Johansen's method is that it accounts for simultaneity when testing for relationships among prices. Johansen's method was applied to determine the cointegration rank, r, that defines the number of cointegration vectors among the price series. These cointegration vectors define the stationary linear combinations that represent long-run relationships among prices.[1] EViews software[2] (Quantitative Micro Software 2008) supports two likelihood ratio tests for cointegration rank, trace tests and maximum eigenvalue tests. The trace test statistic with null hypothesis of r cointegrating relations is tested against an alternative of n cointegrating relations for $r = 0,1,\ldots,n - 1$. The maximum eigenvalue test uses the null hypothesis of r cointegrating relations against alternative $r + 1$. The number of cointegrating relations r is determined by testing sequentially from $r = 0$ to $r = n - 1$ until failure to reject.

For two price series, if the number of cointegrated equations equals zero, $r = 0$, prices are not cointegrated, and ordinary least squares in differences can be used in testing. If $r = 2$, the series are individually stationary or the model is misspecified. If $r = 1$, the two series are cointegrated and an error-correction model can be formulated that incorporates the long-run effects.

---

[1] The procedure uses a model that can be reparameterized in error correction form:
$$\Delta P_t = \Gamma_1 \Delta P_{t-1} + ,\ldots, + \Gamma_{k-1} \Delta P_{t-k+1} + \prod P_{t-k} + \mu + \varepsilon_t, \tag{6}$$
where ΔP_t is a $I(0)$ vector, μ is a vector of constant terms, ε_t is a vector of error terms, t is time, and k is lag length. $\prod$ is a matrix of long-run coefficients that can be decomposed into a matrix of loadings, α, and a matrix of cointegration vectors, β. The loadings are adjustment coefficients that describe the speed of adjustment toward the long-run equilibrium state (Hanninen, 1998).

[2] The use of trade or firm names in this publication is for reader information and does not imply endorsement by the U.S. Department of Agriculture for any product or service.

Results

Each of the 62 national forest price series was tested for the presence of a unit root in levels using the Augmented Dickey-Fuller test. Three specifications of the ADF test equation, including an exogenous constant, constant and trend, and neither, were examined for each price series. Lag length in the test regression was selected using the Schwarz Information Criterion with a maximum lag length of 14 quarters. One specification was selected from the three possibilities based upon the statistical significance of the exogenous variables in the test equation. After the initial round of ADF tests, prices with a unit root in levels were tested again in first differences. Results of unit root tests on the levels and first differences for each forest are presented in tables 9 through 12. Lags and exogenous regressors are also provided.

The ADF tests on the level price series in Region 1 (table 9) cannot reject the null hypothesis of a unit root for the Beaverhead, Idaho Panhandle, and Kootenai National Forests. The remaining nine forests in Region 1 had timber prices that were stationary over time. Beaverhead-Deerlodge, Idaho Panhandle, and Kootenai prices were retested after first differencing and found to be stationary, making them $I(1)$ series. Unit root tests on stumpage prices for the 13 forests in Region 4 (table 10) suggest that only the Salmon-Challis prices were nonstationary in levels; these prices were stationary after taking first differences. Table 11 shows that

Table 9—Northern Region Augmented Dickey-Fuller (ADF) unit root test results

Forest	Lags	c/t	ADF test statistic	P-value
Levels:				
Beaverhead-Deerlodge	2	c	-2.272542	0.1831[a]
Bitterroot	0	c	-7.400908	0.0000
Clearwater	0	c	-7.483048	0.0000
Custer	0	c/t	-9.079930	0.0000
Flathead	0	c	-8.310932	0.0000
Gallatin	0	c/t	-7.649239	0.0000
Helena	0	c	-8.800348	0.0000
Idaho Panhandle	1	c	-2.354934	0.1575[a]
Kootenai	1	c	-2.277512	0.1814[a]
Lewis and Clark	0	c	-6.330181	0.0000
Lolo	1	c	-3.516631	0.0096
Nez Perce	0	c	-8.453381	0.0000
Differenced:				
Beaverhead-Deerlodge	1	c	-11.64789	0.0000
Idaho Panhandle	1	c	-9.802014	0.0000
Kootenai	0	c	-14.43330	0.0000

H_0: price series has a unit root.
[a] 5-percent critical values are -3.46 if both constant (c) and trend (t) are significant, -2.89 if only c or t is significant, and -1.95 if neither is significant.

Table 10—Intermountain Region Augmented Dickey-Fuller (ADF) unit root test results

Forest	Lags	c/t	ADF test statistic	P-value
Levels:				
Ashley	0	c/t	-9.138389	0.0000
Boise	0	c	-4.528322	0.0004
Bridger-Teton	0	c	-7.100780	0.0000
Caribou-Targhee	0	c/t	-5.947208	0.0000
Dixie	0	c	-8.097313	0.0000
Fishlake	0	c/t	-9.032938	0.0000
Humboldt-Toiyabe	7	c	-4.348650	0.0007
Manti-La Sal	0	c	-10.40103	0.0000
Payette	0	c	-4.278887	0.0009
Salmon-Challis	1	c	-2.828698	0.0582[a]
Sawtooth	0	c/t	-6.616439	0.0000
Uinta	0	c/t	-7.859380	0.0000
Wasatch-Cache	0	c	-7.189601	0.0000
Differenced:				
Salmon-Challis	1	c	-10.79841	0.0000

H_0:price series has a unit root.
[a] 5-percent critical values are -3.46 if both constant (c) and trend (t) are significant, -2.89 if only c or t is significant, and -1.95 if neither is significant.

Table 11—Pacific Southwest Region Augmented Dickey-Fuller (ADF) unit root test results

Forest	Lags	c/t	ADF test statistic	P-value
Levels:				
Angeles	0	c/t	-7.642664	0.0000
Cleveland	0	c	-9.687432	0.0000
Eldorado	0	c/t	-6.524876	0.0000
Inyo	0	c/t	-8.617902	0.0000
Klamath	2	—	-0.677211	0.4210[a]
LTBMA[b]	1	c	-4.774505	0.0002
Lassen	0	c/t	-8.322066	0.0000
Los Padres	0	c	-5.577216	0.0000
Mendocino	0	c/t	-7.661781	0.0000
Modoc	0	c/t	-10.19368	0.0000
Plumas	1	c/t	-3.773725	0.0224
San Bernardino	0	c/t	-7.210926	0.0000
Sequoia	0	c	-4.814435	0.0001
Shasta-Trinity	0	c	-6.354482	0.0000
Sierra	0	c/t	-7.320846	0.0000
Six Rivers	0	c/t	-5.845587	0.0000
Stanislaus	0	c/t	-6.929840	0.0000
Tahoe	0	c/t	-4.456949	0.0030
Differenced:				
Klamath	4	c	-8.030741	0.0000

H_0:price series has a unit root; — = neither c or t were used in the regression equation.
[a] 5-percent critical values are -3.46 if both constant (c) and trend (t) are significant, -2.89 if only c or t is significant, and -1.95 if neither is significant.
[b] LTBMA is the Lake Tahoe Basin Management Area.

Table 12—Pacific Northwest Region Augmented Dickey-Fuller (ADF) unit root test results

Forest	Lags	c/t	ADF test statistic	P-value
Levels:				
Colville	0	c	-6.697005	0.0000
Deschutes	0	c/t	-8.182768	0.0000
Fremont	0	c/t	-5.954486	0.0000
Gifford Pinchot	0	c/t	-7.445691	0.0000
Malheur	0	c/t	-7.069117	0.0000
Mount Baker-Snoqualmie	0	c/t	-4.842384	0.0009
Mount Hood	2	c	-1.890142	0.3356[a]
Ochoco	0	c/t	-8.631505	0.0000
Okanogan	0	c	-6.348353	0.0000
Olympic	0	c/t	-6.370327	0.0000
Rogue River	3	c/t	-3.522482	0.0430
Siskiyou	0	c	-7.167214	0.0000
Siuslaw	1	c	-3.948818	0.0026
Umatilla	0	c	-7.274883	0.0000
Umpqua	0	c/t	-5.020876	0.0004
Wallowa-Whitman	1	c	-3.324856	0.0165
Wenatchee	0	c	-6.510945	0.0000
Willamette	0	c/t	-5.109568	0.0003
Winema	0	c/t	-8.939931	0.0000
Differenced:				
Mount Hood	1	—	-12.37289	0.0000

H_0:price series has a unit root; — = neither c or t were used in the regression equation.
[a] 5-percent critical values are -3.46 if both constant (c) and trend (t) are significant, -2.89 if only c or t is significant, and -1.95 if neither is significant.

the Klamath National Forest in Region 5 has nonstationary stumpage prices that became stationary after first differencing. Region 6 also had predominantly stationary stumpage prices; of the 19 national forests in Washington and Oregon, only the Mount Hood had nonstationary prices (table 12). The Mount Hood series was tested after first differencing and a unit root was rejected. Thus, of 62 forests tested, only stumpage prices on the Beaverhead-Deerlodge, Idaho Panhandle, Kootenai, Salmon-Challis, Klamath, and Mount Hood were nonstationary $I(1)$ processes. The map in figure 7 shows the spatial arrangement of the six forests with nonstationary prices.

Cointegration tests to detect market integration were performed on the Beaverhead-Deerlodge, Idaho Panhandle, Kootenai, and Salmon-Challis National Forests. The Klamath and Mount Hood National Forests were excluded from testing because of their isolated locations. The test specification allowed for a linear deterministic trend in the data and an intercept in the cointegrating equation. Tests were conducted using from one to four lags; results were the same, so one lag was chosen

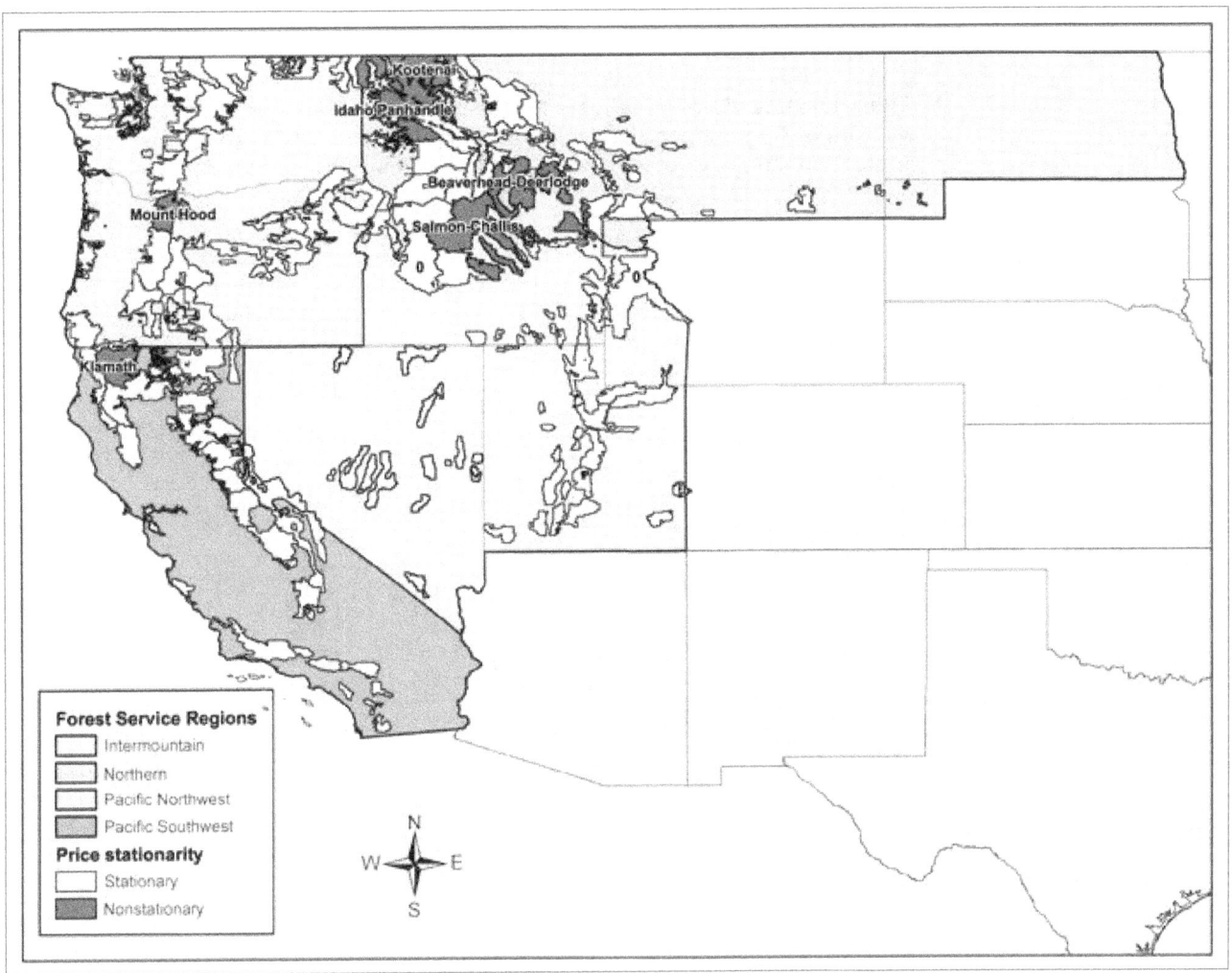

Figure 7—National forests with nonstationary stumpage prices.

for model parsimony. Both the trace and the maximal eigenvalue tests rejected the hypothesis of no cointegration ($r = 0$). The trace (table 13) and maximal eigenvalue (table 14) tests agreed that there was evidence of two cointegrating equations at the 0.05 level. Pairwise tests were then used to identify which forests were fully integrated. Test results indicated that the four forests can be grouped into two sets of integrated markets. The Beaverhead-Deerlodge and Salmon-Challis compose one market while the Idaho Panhandle and the Kootenai make up the other (fig. 8).

Table 13—Results of trace tests for the number of cointegration vectors (*r*) for stumpage prices on the Beaverhead-Deerlodge, Idaho Panhandle, Kootenai, and Salmon-Challis National Forests

Null hypothesis	Lags	Eigenvalue	Trace statistic	Critical value	P-value
r = 0	1	0.4470	112.5023	63.8761	0.0000
r ≤ 1		0.3347	58.5926	42.9152	0.0007
r ≤ 2		0.1760	21.5038	25.8721	0.1590
r ≤ 3		0.0418	3.8875	12.5180	0.7583

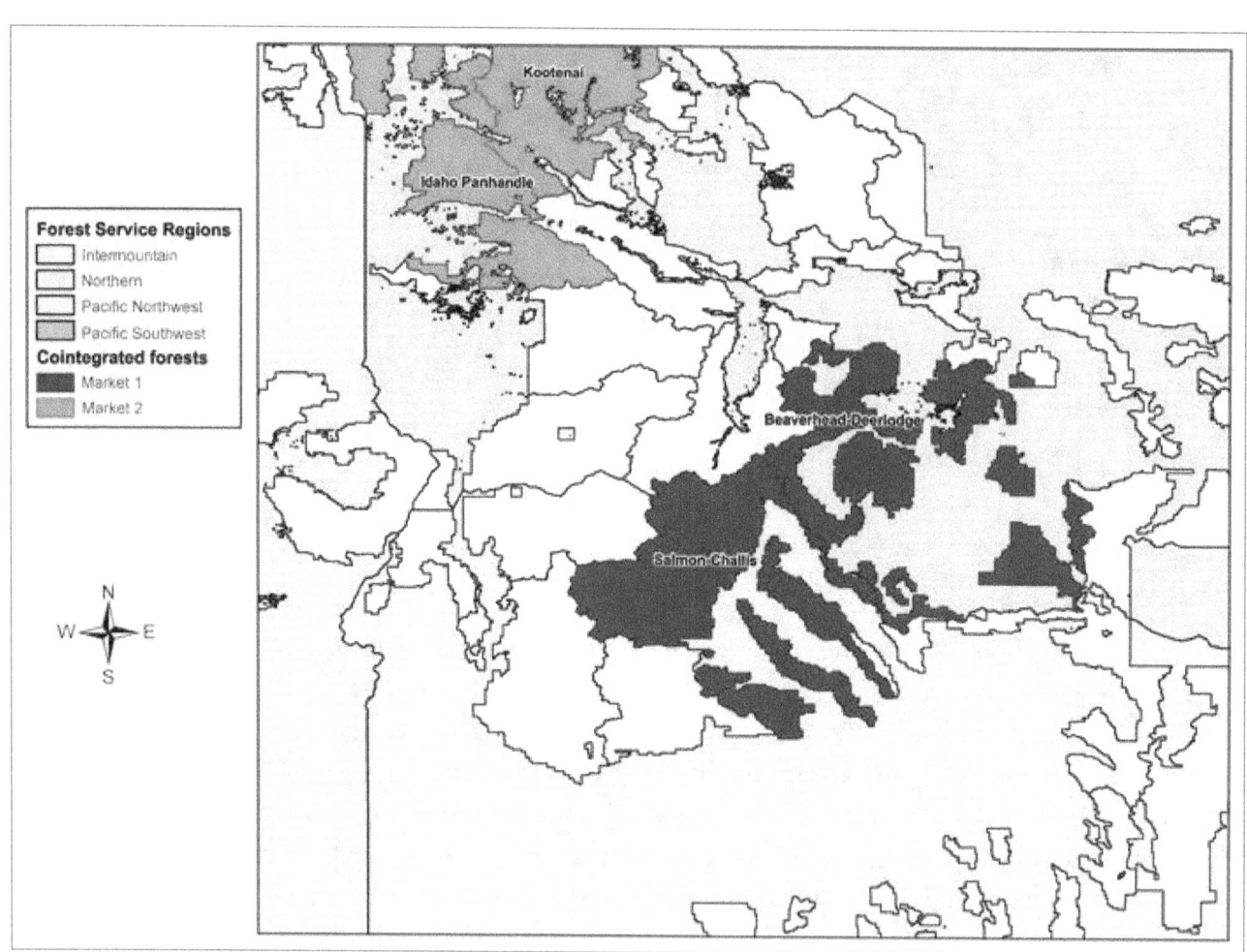

Figure 8—National forests with cointegrated stumpage markets.

Table 14—Results of maximal eigenvalue tests for the number of cointegration vectors (*r*) for stumpage prices on the Beaverhead-Deerlodge, Idaho Panhandle, Kootenai, and Salmon-Challis National Forests

Null hypothesis	Lags	Eigenvalue	Max-eigen statistic	Critical value	P-value
$r = 0$	1	0.4470	53.9098	32.1183	0.0000
$r \leq 1$		0.3347	37.0888	25.8232	0.0011
$r \leq 2$		0.1760	17.6162	19.3870	0.0887
$r \leq 3$		0.0418	3.8875	12.5179	0.7583

Conclusion and Direction of Future Research

This analysis suggests that 4 of the 62 national forests in the Western United States belong to two fully integrated stumpage markets. There is no evidence to support aggregation beyond these two markets. The majority of stumpage prices were stationary; market integration and the law of one price were rejected in 58 cases. Other than the two markets comprising the Beaverhead-Deerlodge and Salmon-Challis Forests and the Idaho Panhandle and Kootenai Forests, the LOP was rejected in every case, suggesting that arbitrage opportunities exist for national forest timber purchasers. There is no single regional market but instead a collection of independent localized markets reflecting greater differentiation than expected or modeled in the past.

Although Yin and Newman (1996) found stationarity in the 14 stumpage markets they examined in the U.S. South, price time series are rarely stationary (Stevens and Brooks 2003). Stationarity implies mean reversion; the influence of changes dissipates with time and prices converge back to a steady state. One possible explanation for stationary stumpage prices across the West is informational inefficiency of stumpage markets (Yin and Newman 1996). Errors and inefficiencies in stumpage pricing do not persist in price patterns, so potential purchasers do not receive the market signals necessary to capture potential gains. Even great price run-ups experienced in the early 1990s (Sohngen and Haynes 1994) do not persist; prices slowly decay back to their original level and purchasers cannot be confident that one windfall period will persist or be followed by another. Another possibility is that prices are determined by a bid process. Each timber sale and the timber price associated with the winning bid could be considered an independent event that is uncorrelated with time and previous sales.

Managers on the Beaverhead-Deerlodge, Salmon-Challis, Idaho Panhandle, and Kootenai National Forests should be aware that one implication of integrated stumpage markets is that policies that change prices of stumpage in one forest may lead to changes in others. These unintended consequences may arise because the markets are not independent (Nanang 2000). This could be especially problematic for the Beaverhead-Deerlodge and Salmon-Challis Forests, as they are administered by different Forest Service regions.

And last, anyone conducting statistical tests using national forest stumpage prices is cautioned to conduct analyses only after first differencing prices. Time series processes with a unit root are prone to appear to trend over time, but this trend is entirely spurious. One way to prevent this problem is to take first differences before estimating regression models. This removes correlation among error terms over time, resulting in unbiased parameter estimates. This again is why it is so important to account for price stationarity as a precautionary measure to avoid erroneous results.

Future efforts will incorporate the surprising results reported here into the spatial pricing model. Since most of the prices were stationary, vector error-correction (VEC) models that account for cross-forest interactions only need to be included in two cases. Developing these VEC models is the next step in model formation. Then, the relationship between distance to wood product manufacturing clusters and stumpage prices will be examined for each forest. Afterwards, the relationship between sawtimber and nonsawtimber prices will be estimated for each forest, using export chip prices as a proxy for nonsawtimber (Busby 2006). Finally, a forest-level spreadsheet tool will be developed that asks for input on the percentage of sawtimber, nonsawtimber, and firewood to be harvested from a timber sale and allow the user to vary these percentages until the total value is expected to be great enough to entice purchasers. The hope is that the tool will assist forest managers by increasing the likelihood that advertised sales will contain the right combination of timber sizes to be profitable for potential purchasers while accomplishing management objectives.

Acknowledgments

Many thanks to reviewers Dennis Dykstra, Richard Haynes, John Perez-Garcia, and Stanislav Petrasek for their comments and input, Judy Mikowski and Lynn Sullivan for assistance in manuscript preparation, and John Chase for assistance with the maps. Funded through National Fire Plan Portfolio E. Any errors are solely my responsibility.

References

Adams, D.M.; Haynes, R.W. 1996. The 1993 timber assessment market model: structure, projections, and policy simulations. Gen. Tech. Rep. PNW-GTR-368. Portland, OR: U.S. Department of Agriculture, Forest Service, Pacific Northwest Research Station. 58 p.

Alavalapati, J.R.R.; Adamowicz, W.L.; Luckert, M.K. 1997. A cointegration analysis of Canadian wood pulp prices. American Journal of Agricultural Economics. 79: 975–986.

Baek, J. 2006. Price linkages in the North American softwood lumber market. Canadian Journal of Forest Research. 36(6): 1527–1535.

Binkley, C.S.; Dykstra, D.P. 1987. Timber supply. In: Kallio, M.; Dykstra, D.P.; Binkley, C.S., eds. The global forest sector, an analytical perspective. New York: John Wiley and Sons: 508–534.

Busby, G.M. 2006. Export chip prices as a proxy for nonsawtimber prices in the Pacific Northwest log export market. Res. Note PNW-RN-554. Portland, OR: U.S. Department of Agriculture, Forest Service, Pacific Northwest Research Station. 14 p.

Buongiorno, J.; Uusivuori, J. 1992. The law of one price in the trade of forest products: cointegration tests for U.S. exports of pulp and paper. Forest Science. 38(3): 539–553.

Daniels, J.M. 2005. The rise and fall of the Pacific Northwest log export market. Gen. Tech. Rep. PNW-GTR-624. Portland, OR: U.S. Department of Agriculture, Forest Service, Pacific Northwest Research Station. 80 p.

Dickey, D.A.; Fuller, W.A. 1979. Distribution of the estimators for autoregressive time series with a unit root. Journal of the American Statistical Association. 74: 427–431.

Granger, C.S. 1988. Some recent developments in the concept of causality. Journal of Econometrics. 39: 199–211.

Greene, W. 2003. Econometric analysis. 5th ed. Upper Saddle River, NJ: Prentice Hall. 1026 p.

Hanninen, R. 1998. The law of one price in United Kingdom soft sawnwood imports—a cointegration approach. Forest Science. 44(1): 17–23.

Hanninen, R.; Toppinen, A.; Ruuska, P. 1997. Testing arbitrage in newsprint imports to United Kingdom and Germany. Canadian Journal of Forest Research. 27: 1946–1952.

Johansen, S. 1995. Likelihood-based inference in cointegrated vector autoregressive models. New York: Oxford University Press. 267 p.

Jung, C.; Doroodian, K. 1994. The law of one price for U.S. softwood lumber: a multivariate cointegration test. Forest Science. 40(4): 595–600.

Kling, D. 2008. Stumpage prices and volumes sold for individual western national forests. Res. Note PNW-RN-558. Portland, OR: U.S. Department of Agriculture, Forest Service, Pacific Northwest Research Station. 57 p.

Luppold, W.; Baumgras, J. 1996. Relationship between hardwood lumber and sawlog prices: a case study of Ohio 1975–1994. Forest Products Journal. 46: 35–40.

Luppold, W.; Prestemon, J.; Baumgras, J. 1998. An examination of the relationships between hardwood lumber and stumpage prices in Ohio. Wood Fiber Science. 30: 281–292.

Murray, B.; Wear, D. 1998. Federal timber restrictions and interregional arbitrage in U.S. lumber. Land Economics. 74(1): 76–91.

Nagubadi, V.; Munn, I.A.; Ahai, A. 2001. Integration of hardwood stumpage markets in the Southcentral United States. Journal of Forest Economics. 7(1): 69–98.

Nanang, D.M. 2000. A multivariate cointegration test of the law of one price for Canadian softwood lumber markets. Forest Policy and Economics. 1: 347–355.

Prestemon, J. 2003. Evaluation of U.S. southern pine stumpage market informational efficiency. Canadian Journal of Forest Research. 33(4): 561–572.

Prestemon, J.; Holmes, T. 2000. Timber price dynamics following a natural catastrophe. American Journal of Agricultural Economics. 82: 145–160.

Quantitative Micro Software. 2008. EViews 6 software and user's guide. Irvine, CA.

Riis, J. 1996. Forecasting Danish timber prices with an error correction model. Journal of Forest Economics. 2: 257–271.

Shahi, C.; Kant, S.; Yang, F. 2006. The law of one price in the North American softwood lumber markets. Forest Science. 52(4): 353–366.

Sohngen, B.; Haynes, R. 1994. The "great" price spike of '93: an analysis of lumber and stumpage prices in the Pacific Northwest. Res. Pap. PNW-RP-476. Portland, OR: U.S. Department of Agriculture, Forest Service, Pacific Northwest Research Station. 20 p.

Stevens, J.A.; Brooks, D.J. 2003. Alaska softwood market price arbitrage. Res. Pap. PNW-RP-556. Portland, OR: U.S. Department of Agriculture, Forest Service, Pacific Northwest Research Station. 12 p.

Stordal, S.; Nyrud, A. 2003. Testing roundwood market efficiency using a multivariate cointegration estimator. Forest Policy and Economics. 5: 57–68.

Tang, X.; Laaksonen-Craig, S. 2007. The law of one price in the United States and Canadian newsprint markets. Canadian Journal of Forest Research. 37: 1495–1504.

Thorsen, B.J. 1998. Spatial integration in the Nordic timber market: long-run equilibria and short-run dynamics. Scandinavian Journal of Forest Resources. 13(4): 382–389.

Thorsen, B.J.; Riis, J.; Helles, F.; Holten-Anderson, P. 1999. Internationalisation of roundwood markets: the case of Denmark. In: Abildrup, J.; Helles, F.; Holten-Anderson, P.; Larsen, J.F.; Thorsen, B.J., eds. Modern time series analysis in forest products markets. Boston, MA: Kluwer Academic Publishers: 69–81.

Toivonen, R.; Toppinen, A.; Tilli, T. 2002. Integration of roundwood markets in Austria, Finland, and Sweden. Forest Policy and Economics. 4: 33–42.

Toppinen, A.; Toivonen, R. 1998. Roundwood market integration in Finland: a multivariate cointegration analysis. Journal of Forest Economics. 4(3): 241–266.

Uri, N.D.; Boyd, R.G. 1990. Considerations on modeling the market for softwood lumber in the United States. Forest Science. 36(3): 680–692.

Yin, R.; Newman, D.H. 1996. Are markets for stumpage informationally efficient. Canadian Journal of Forest Research. 26: 1032–1039.

Yin, R.; Xu, J. 2003. Identifying the inter-market relationships of forest products in the Pacific Northwest with cointegration and causality tests. Forest Policy and Economics. 5(3): 305–315.

Zhou, M.; Buongiorno, J. 2005. Price transmission between products at different stages of manufacturing in forest industries. Journal of Forest Economics. 11: 5–19.